CHIMERA

T0282019

Also by Phoebe Giannisi
From New Directions

Cicada

CHIMERA

Phoebe Giannisi

Translated from the Modern Greek by
Brian Sneeden

A New Directions Book

The photograph on page 9 is courtesy of Chara Stergiou.

Manufactured in the United States of America
First published as New Directions Paperbook 1606 in 2024.

Library of Congress Cataloging-in-Publication Data
Names: Giannisē, Phoivē, author. | Sneeden, Brian, translator.
Title: Chimera / Phoebe Giannisi ; translated from the Modern Greek by Brian Sneeden.
Other titles: Chimaira. English
Description: New York : New Directions Publishing Corporation, 2024. | "A New Directions book"
Identifiers: LCCN 2024008829 | ISBN 9780811237826 (paperback) | ISBN 9780811237833 (ebook)
Subjects: LCGFT: Poetry.
Classification: LCC PA5638.17.I1885 C4813 2024 | DDC 889.1/4—dc23/eng/20240317
LC record available at https://lccn.loc.gov/2024008829

10 9 8 7 6 5 4 3 2 1

New Directions Books are published for James Laughlin
by New Directions Publishing Corporation
80 Eighth Avenue, New York 10011

for Kaiti, my mother

χίμαιρ-α
chimera, *f.*

I.   she-goat, sacrificed before the battle to the goddess
     Artemis; wild goat; young female goat; a kid.

II. a. legendary fire-breathing creature with the body of a she-
        goat, the head of a lion, and the tail of a dragon.
     b. name of a volcano in the Cragus Mountains of Lycia.

III. in modern Greek, a metonym for a fantastical creature,
     a vain daydream, an unfulfilled desire, a utopia, a self-
     deception.

IV. in modern Greek, a botanical term, a graft, what is made
     from joining a rootstock and scion.

Since the end of the twentieth century, our age, a legendary
age, we're all chimeras, theoretical and created hybrids from
machine and organism; in short, we're all cyborgs.

                    —*Donna Haraway,* A Cyborg Manifesto

Microchimerism (Mc) refers to an individual hosting a small
number of cells or DNA that come from a different individual.
It was first observed in humans when cells containing the
male Y chromosome were found in the blood of women after
giving birth. Being genetically male, the cells couldn't belong
to the women bearing them, so it was assumed they originated
in the embryos during pregnancy. In a recent study, however,
scientists noticed that the microchimeric cells in some women
didn't just circulate in the blood, but also integrated for several

years inside the brain. The prevalence, diversity, and durability of the naturally obtained Mc in healthy individuals shows that a change must be made in the conventional way of thinking of the self as individual, to one that conceptualizes the self as a chimera composed of many parts.

—from various online sources

The poem, then, is a speech for two (*Gespräch*, joint-speech), a speech for more than one, a speech that contains more than one inside it, a speech that collects more than one "I."

—Jacques Derrida

XAΊPE ZΏON

HELLO ANIMAL[*]

*   Welcome-screen message on one of the narrator's first mobile phones,
Nokia series (circa 2000). Animal: ζῷον (*zoon*), from life (ζωή, *zoe*), creature,
living thing.

the narrator says:

goatfold of Yannis Mourtos in Kalamaki Larissa.
750 stock, 700 females. goats.

two winters I went among the fold with Chara
I saw the animals scream and fuck
                    (when the human let them)
I saw the animals being born
                    (with the help of the human)
I saw the animals graze
                    (led by the human)
animals shorn and adorned
                    (when the human wanted it)
I saw the animals slaughtered and skinned
separated from their mothers.
Life and death together
determined
by the human that does unto them
as a god.

Noon

a row of cypresses towered over the road
we knelt at the water's source
drank its cleanness.
plane trees shaded the ground. shaded
the brown-on-brown tufts. wool from shearing
residue of hands on the bodies of animals.
at Easter the ditchwater purples
while in the square, huddled together, awaiting
sacrifice, the chosen offering
bleats.
flesh
prey for humans
shared with wine.
wine blood. wine bread.
dirt.
"A soul dressed in a body," Empedocles says,
earth surrounding the mortal
earth surrounding the death-susceptible
earth surrounding the already gone.

1. DOGS

Narrator: How many dogs have you got in your herd? There's what, 700 goats?

Uncle Yannis: Mine? 13 dogs.

Pouqueville says:

The dogs that belong to the Vlach shepherds are Molossian hounds, fearless, eyes lit with a kind of fire, their pricked ears catching even the slightest sound, vigilant sentinels, friends of the hearth, the family, their masters for whom they would give everything. They step proudly at the front of the herd, which they contain without even once showing their fangs. They contain the land, watchful of wolves, which they attack, and they nearly always emerge victorious.

> *Goatself:*
>
> to learn about the goats
> I spoke with the shepherd.
> he belonged to a nomadic people.
> spring on the mountain
> fall in the valley.
> he was a seaman,
> when he retired he came back
> to the herd.
> he was strict
> he cursed politicians.
> I asked him for his dog
> he said not a chance.
> there was no way
> he'd ever
> give it to me.

William Martin Leake says:

The shepherds of Kipinas would sometimes graft a fragment of bone from a dog's foot, about two inches long, into the side of a grown sheep. They would open up the flesh, place the bone

in, and sew up the wound. This procedure had two benefits:
it fortified the stamina of the sheep for the mountain's harsh
weather, and it also callused the flesh, imparting a foul smell
that repelled wolves.

> *Goatself:*
>
> to learn about the goats
> I took from the shepherd
> his dog.
> now it lives with me in the city.
> it's good with strangers
> though sometimes it can be
> a little aggressive.
> but out of affection
> because I am both
> the shepherd that feeds it
> and the goat
> it must guard.

Edward Daniel Clarke says:

In East Katerini I met a group of Arnaut shepherds armed with
large pistols and knives. It was strange to us, how they clothed
their sheepdogs to keep them from the cold.

> *Goatself:*
>
> you said I am your goat
> and you are my dog.

the narrator asks:

how old is it?

shepherd:

one
a little acorn this
just a pup. We tossed it in with the goats to know them,
see how it plays, how it paws the dirt.

> *narrator:*
>
> hay clinging to its back
> eyes laughing
> rolling on the dirt floor of the pen
> curling up.

Yannis Tsevrechos says:

I emptied my rucksack, and what food I had I offered to one
of my cousin's dogs I found watching over two newborn kids.
Throughout the night it laid curled so the goats could nestle
against its belly.

> *Goatself:*
>
> caring for another saves you
> from your dominant self.

Yannis Tsevrechos says:

Their feeding time is before the herd is let out to graze and
after they come back. At the day's start and close, the dog is the
first and last concern.

the narrator says:

for centuries they fed the dogs
black bread made from bran. not yeast.
and in the same basin where
they kneaded the dogbread
women gave birth
if a baby came during
the walking season.

Giorgos the biologist says:

dogs and wolves
are classified under the same genus
—they used to list them separately, nature/civilization—
those that could digest starch
the humans took with them
to eat bread—like them.

Leonidas the historian says:

wolves worship the strong
the breed bows its head
hence domestication.

     dialogue between the shepherd and narrator:

    —That dog took on a bear up the mountain,
      got his tendon torn up. That's why he limps.
    —What's his name?
    —Davelis. Like the bandit. A warrior. Yet he's the
      quietest one. Just lies around.

Dimitris Loukopoulos the folklorist says:

somewhere out there the sheepdog
opens and closes its eyes.
and the shepherd farther off
in the thick shade of a fir tree or perhaps a cedar
lying on his belly or his back, depending on the moods of sleep
drinks the polished air of ridge
and wood.

> *Goatself:*
>
> I'm accompanied by
> that most yours
> and delicate
> first voice.
> I'm accompanied by your breath.

Loukopoulos says:

in the deepest shade
the shepherd sleeps
on his back
the dog sleeps
everywhere, a solitude and stillness.

> *Goatself:*
>
> always it comes
> following behind—to sleep beside me
> to place
> its head on my thigh
> thigh—head
> a new double animal
> companioned.

18

Homer says, the translators struggling:

ἀπόθεστος
δὴ τότε κεῖτ᾽ ἀπόθεστος (εκ του θέσσασθαι)
and so he laid there scorned
and unseen, no one called for him
ἀποιχομένοιο Ἄνακτος
and when his master was away
he lay unseen and scorned
before the palace door
where the shit of mules and oxen
streamed endlessly

ἔνθα κύων κεῖτ᾽ Ἄργος, ἐνίπλειος κυνοραιστέων
Argos the dog laid there, covered in ticks
he who, when he sensed Odysseus approaching,
wagged his tail, lowered his ears
though he lacked the strength to rise and go to him
and Odysseus, seeing him, dried secretly
a tear, and entered straightaway
into the palace.

Goatself:

Argos
from the word *argos*, meaning swift
in Homer's time, now it means slow
the Swift becomes slow
the dog once royal—now a beggar
on the steps of the palace—
through some insight he knew
he too
had taken the guise of his master

and into a beggar
had changed
or maybe it was his master
who chose to enter the house
in the guise of a dog?

the translators:

Ἄργον δ᾽ αὖ κατὰ μοῖρ᾽ ἔλαβεν μέλανος θανάτοιο, αὐτίκ᾽ ἰδόντ᾽
Ὀδυσῆα ἐεικοστῷ ἐνιαυτῷ.
and after twenty years of waiting for Odysseus
and finally laying eyes on him, death seized Argos.

Goatself:

waiting by the door
for years, until he'd grown old, until
he was prepared to die
waiting, and when his master came
no one
but he recognized,
the dog and slave who
on seeing him wagged
his tail, tried to stand
and let his soul out
with its small heart
which had for so long
companied.

Prelude: Gray March Sky

Each spring I give again the burial of myself.
I bury the others, the previous springs
I bury this spring, which is not like the rest
I bury myself in spring
so that I may crawl inside my body in summer
and tear from the desiccated hide of autumn
and winter, stubbornly, to insist the ghost
of my compulsion
winter would have absolute freedom
existence in the vast expanse
of Mongolian highlands, the gallop
of long-haired horses, the words
of singers from another season, storytellers
but—
as when at the end of winter, in the fatigue and exhaustion
of daily regimen
a star flashes suddenly in the sky
of the cup of wine we are drinking
in solitude together
and the star's glint leading us astray
down old paths, driving us to open once more
we owe this opening, the paths nearly closed
from branches and ferns
we owe this abandonment
again and again each year we bury
what we were and leave behind
an exoskeleton of singular form
each different but multiple
we bury it with ritual in the grasses
we leave it in the bright stems
of weeds it clung to, we rip it out
we bury it in the sand, we toss it in the sea

on the way we meet women carrying bouquets
of wildflowers, gazing off. slowly
and tortuously we begin to clear the paths
there in the middle space of the half-opened
beneath the earth, in myriad creatures
spring is sleeping.

2. EARTH

Yannis Mourtos, owner of the herd, shepherd ever since he was a boy: This one time, guys, we had a place in Grevena. It was so muddy that if we got caught in the rain, our shoes would peel off. The ground was heavy clay, and if it was raining you were stuck. When we made it to Kalirachi the next morning, the women would say, "Sleep well?" "Shut up." Why? Because of all the mud!

X: The mud was very sticky.

X2: And what kind of shoes were you wearing again?

YM: What kind of shoes. Pig-tsarouchia! Pork-leather.

Yannis Mourtos shares a proverb:

what the goat does to the holly, the holly does to the goat
or
what the goat inflicts on the holly shrub will be told on the
       goat's skin
meaning
what you do to others will happen to you.

The tanner says:

goats are tough, they eat hollies.
but the hollies are barbed, which scrapes their skin
and leaves cuts and gouges we find later
when the goat is processed
in other words
the skin is a canvas, the skin is earth.

William Martin Leake says:

Those villages mostly get by making a rough woolen fabric
called *skouti* that is then used to created overcoats, called
kappais—*cappe* in Italian—worn widely in Greece and the
Adriatic. The fabric is of two colors: white and black, and the
inner part is a coarse wool sent to Venice and Trieste in lengths
called masts.

Panagiotis the cheese maker says:

my *yaya* used to weave, she had a loom
we threw away a few years ago
because no one used it anymore.

narrator:

in this place

the earth's surface

a carpet woven

from human animals

humanimals

the carpet of earth

eternally woven

for time to tear apart

timeweather tears apart what humans animals weave

time and animals within the ground

the weave of man

undone.

Panagiotis the cheese maker says:

my *yaya* was tall and thin but very strong
could shake out the heavy wool carpets by herself
after washing, like it was nothing. When she was widowed
she climbed the mountain by herself
with the herd and the children too.

the narrator says:

the goats eat: oak, acorn, strawberry tree, grass, broom,
Cornelian cherry, blackthorn, wool, dog rose, thorn apple, pear,
wild vines, firs.

Makis M., former breeder, says:

I knew a shepherd once who went foraging on the mountain
and ate by accident the berries of a belladonna, so-called
because women in Europe put drops made from it in their
eyes, to dilate their pupils, so their gaze was more intense. He
stumbled down the mountain with his axe. Tried to kill his
children. But they dragged him to a hospital and tied him up,
and for a full day he whistled and called out, poor man, for his
goats and dogs.

> *Goatself:*
>
> hours by myself
> I dream
> leaping here and there
> I choose a branch
> and chew
> branch by branch
> step by step.
> I choose the sky.

Pouqueville says:

The herds descend the mountain's slope in undulating lines,
one can see the clatter of their hooves and hear their bells—the
tsokani bells of male goats, the *trokani* bells of the females, the
rams, and the sheep—in miraculous harmony.

Makis M., former breeder, says:

Another time there was what we call a *gisemi*, a castrated ram, and they gave it a large bell to make noise with, we called it the *tuba*, it made this metallic jingling sound, it was spring and they were going up to the pastures, and the brush was so thick you could hardly hear the smaller bells, and if a goat ran off into the thicket even two hundred yards away, it was lost forever. But if you had one of those bells on it, the sound travels, a huge echo, penetrating, and you can follow where it goes, so they would put it on the *gisemi* in spring to help them find it. It's their GPS.

William Martin Leake says:

On its south side, from where we entered, the town ends at a precipitous cliff, close enough to the opposite side on the ridge that voices could be heard across from the church there, the Agios Georgios. As if this is the first surveillance transmitted when travelers or caravans come from Ioannina… It's a strange thing, how much the communication owes to telelalia, to speaking from a distance. It's an art, like *telescopia*, which is recognizing things that are far away, something the Albanians and mountain-dwelling Greeks have refined.

> *Goatself:*
>
> the pillow:
> I made a mountain
> and fell on it to sleep.

A Vlach song, sung by girls, goes:

Where will we stay tonight?
Behind the sea
a caravan passes
laden with salt
and a grand young man
on a horse
with his elegant combed hair
and waxen mustache.

Iris says:

eros. agape.
love.

the breeder says:

And a goat that had left the herd during the night came over
and right there two meters away it says "baaah baaah." He was
on his period. Testosterone. "That" was what it sought. It made
these cries from deep within. Like those of a bear, guttural—a
bear's growls. That's what the goat was looking for. Its sounds
came from inside.

> *Goatself:*
>
> you carry everywhere your own
> piece of dark
> the skin of your living blood
> silent
> shredded in stillness
> pillow

      dreamtank
      drips of poison
      within the body
      unseen
      ἀεὶ πολεῖ.

the other song goes:

the girl from the east and the boy from the west,
two strangers, met in a strange place.
"You're a stranger and I'm a stranger,
come, let us spend the night together."

      Goatself:

      me I was born
      of the sea.
      they stuffed my mouth
      with earth
      from the mountain.

you:

you're beautiful
like that.
like a goat

      perched
      on top of me.

      Goatself:

      I'm the goat
      you're the mountain slope.

Matsi:

goats are rocks come to life.

           Goatself:

           a laughing wave.

narrator:

are they any different:
rocks of the mountain
and rocks of the sea?
the same shepherd scales them.

Noon

from a distance we could hear the wild galloping
of hooves on asphalt. we turned our heads
struggling to see through the trees. then
after we got onto the freeway
they overtook us. violent joy
reddened their faces. steam rising
from their strong bodies running.
in their purple beadwork.
their proud straight tails. their vast inexplicable
eyes. for a brief moment I manage
a glimpse of their thighs shining moving.
holding deep inside them
the sun. for the third time midsummer
unfolded red roses at our house.
sometimes I can't stand the thought of what
waits for me.
let it come let the unexpected
find me. a wind.
no one will be able to say with words
where it passes.
a scent.

Dusk

walking in the woods in summer we came upon
loggers. we heard them before we saw them
before we saw them we came upon their traces
walls of logs stacked by the side
of the road waiting for transport
freshly cut trees.
and the bare patch where their bundles
bundles of lithe, young chestnut trees
left behind clearings following their slaughter
before we saw them we heard their voices. distant
and esoteric in the expanse of the shaded wood
why too this sound of bells?
ringing as they climbed the ravine
and turned onto the road
then a rustling of leaves in the low branches
hooves. voice
and you passed like lightning out in front
first the neck glinting with blue talismans
the four black feet and last
the bright eyes of your flaxen head
a second horse hauled lumber. riderless
then the centaur was lost
in the black wood's thicket
our dog followed them at a distance before turning back
you can only follow a dream so far.

Dusk

for Maria and Andreas

a bald spot on the mountain high up.
warmed by the sun before dusk.
as I enter the clearing a young fox
jumps to its feet and runs off
sheltering in mountain ferns.
blueberries are ripe. I wrest a few
from the horse and plop them in
my mouth two at a time. each has its own
flavor. even those that grow side by side.
one more sour. more sweet. bittersweet.
near the sea we found koumara berries.
on the beach beneath the trees
sleep. contentment's incense
weighs our eyelids.
stay with me Oneiros stay
don't leave me with Hypnos alone
I want to fly with you a while tonight
over lands over waters
mountains. seas.

Dusk

I saw the farrier as he was finishing up
the last horseshoe on his knees beneath the horse
filing
with its left hind leg over his shoulder.
he wore a leather apron. he was handsome.
then he gathered his tools and devices
and climbed into the truck. his dog next to him barely a hand-
　　　　length.
in the shop the saddle maker
with axe and adze works
the goatskin lays out the skeleton with trinkets
floor submersed in straw. torn saddles littering
a string of lilting consonants from his mouth
bird's beak. cadenced mountain-speak
when he talks on his cell phone I understand nothing
leading astray the mule drivers and the shepherds
the belled saddles of the animals
bear the burden. always
singing ensconced.

3. THE HERD

Uncle Yannis: Because there's love there for humans. Because I lived with them, so, I love them. Ask anyone in this line of work. It's a hard trade, this. I don't know. Ask me anything about breeding, and I can tell you. Anything! There's nothing. 'Cause since my birth, since I started, I was in it. When I climbed up on the horse, the goats came over, all seven hundred of them. When it got dark and I made a fire, the goats would gather round. There's no science to these things. Don't need one. The science of veterinary medicine is death.

X (a goatherd): No science. Only practice. Practice teaches.

Andreas Moukas, from Mt. Parnassus, says:

to call the goats in the morning, we shout: *hei hei hei, tou tou*
        tou tou, tsoi, iou prts, hei hei
and to get them out the pen we call: *hei hei hei, p p p p,*
        (whistling with his fingers), *pr pr pr pr, fr fr fr fr, k k k k,*
        hei hei hei, tso, tr tr, ye-he-he-he
and when we want them to back off: *ha pro tsoi ts ts ts tso*
when it's time to feed them salt: *tsoup tsoup tsoup tsoup, pr tsoi,*
        pr tsoi, ts tsoi, he he-he-hei, hei hei tsoi, pr tsoi
to gather them: *he-he-he-he-he yo-he-he-he ts ts tso he-he he hei hei,*
        strou strou, stro strou stro tsp tsp tsp tsp (whistling with his
        fingers), hei hei hei
and to bring them from the pen for milking: *ts ts tsoi.*

Derrida says:

The herd isn't simply a society of animals, the herd is a set of grouped animals, domesticated animals, monitored and controlled and intended for consumption. I've just spoken about domestication, about indoctrination, about appropriation, about the transformation into pets, but there's also livestock; the herd is a group of animals raised with the purpose of being used and consumed by humans.

the shepherd names the herd and its inventory:

shepherded herds:
herd (*kopi,* meaning cut)
herd (*nomi,* meaning pasture, law)
horde (*ordi,* meaning swarm, gang)
herd (*kouradi,* meaning shit, sheared)
lamb herd (*arnokopi*)
lamb herd, ages two and up (*zigourokopi*)
ram herd (*kriarokopi*)
goat herd (*traoukopi*)
herd of females with no milk (*tsagkadokopado*)
herd of females with milk and their nursing young
        (*galarokopado*)
ageli, goat herd, *gidokopi,* little sheep herd
miliorokopi, goat herd of firstborns

specifically goat herds:
katsikia goats and *katsikakia* kids
garbage herd
tsaggades childless mother herd
male *sirko* and male *arseniko*
the early goats *proimadi*

late-born *psimadi* and way-late the latest
vetoulakia little weanlings,
herd of childless goats between the ages of one and two
        weighing over thirty pounds
milioraki, the one-year-old *vetouli*
unfucked *milona sterfomiliora* birthless kid
little *tragaki*, the two-year-old ramlet
trai the three-year-old ramling
males' ages are measured with scissors
from one, two, three snips
mounochia, dickless ram
castrated one, *katsikomonacha*
neutergoat *kopania*
marmara the sterile one
pratara impossible to separate from the sheep
herdfollower
zavatariko sly one and scourer.

Yannis Tsevrechos says:

often the very intelligence of the animal,
of the herd,
doesn't let you make mistakes.

Dimitris Loukopoulos says:

Goats can be a naughty bunch.
Protected by the Devil, they say,
when the goatherd is away.
So you see, what can a goatherd be but another Devil?
It's difficult, you know, to change the mind of a goat.
No other animal is so destructive.
If one takes a branch in its mouth, good luck.

If one happens upon a wheat field, it turns it into a threshing
    floor.
They'll climb into branches and make mincemeat of the trees.
They'll climb onto the shingles and turn them to Swiss cheese.
Always when goats pass through, it's a biblical event.

The General State Archives mention:

All Vlachs and Sarakatsanis should be dispersed to faraway
provinces because each of them, without exception, views
theft as noble and will hide criminals and vouch for alibis,
and because each is connected through family ties to wanted
thieves, each has racial sympathies, and it's considered a virtue
to harbor criminals.

Some proverbs on goats (Loukopoulos again):

A wise man never lets a goat guard his vineyard.

If a donkey eats a vineyard, it will grow back. If a goat eats a
vineyard, it won't grow back. The goat has a venomous tooth.

The goat devours everything. It's because Christ cursed it when
the goatherd refused him water.

The goat later betrayed Jesus to the Jews when he hid among
the herd and they lifted their forelegs and revealed him.

The General State Archives mention:

Their herds should be collected and confined to each village,
or else they should be forced to build sheepfolds near one
another, within earshot, so that the barking of the dogs of one

pen can be heard by other shepherds close by, because they are known to hide thieves out of fear or self-interest.

Terminology of the Vlachs, Giorgis Exarchos says:

Kouanta di entou
Kid's-tail, referring to those who are arrogant and aloof—a kid's tail always sticks upwards.
Hi toutipouti
(unknown)
mou katsikothike, to overstay, to get one's goat
katsikokleftis, petty-goat-thief.

The General State Archives mention:

Thus all tent-dwellers without exception—Sarakatsanis, Vlachs, Gramoustianis—should be required to camp near established villages in order to be monitored by soldiers stationed there, because should they camp far away from the villages, they'll have no qualms hiding thieves, supplying them with gunpowder, new shoes (*tsarouchia*), and whatever else they might need.

She narrates:

> Goat:
>
> female animal of such-and-such genus
> after learning her hooves
> after weaning
> she ruminates her food
> recalls it back into her mouth
> from the stomach to consider it again.

(Become a goat before you speak, my mother said.)

> ravages everything
> in her path
> used for clearing
> unusable fields
> unwanted
> ungovernable
> unsuppressed
> free to climb where she wants
> to leap
> she plows all the earth with her feet
> in heat and thirst crying out.

Giorgos Giannisis the biologist says:

In all ruminants, the upper incisors are missing. So the jaw
has adapted, resulting in a kind of callus (*tiloma*) in the upper
part. Similarly the lips and tongue have adapted in order to
gather the grass and bring it into the mouth. A characteristic
all species share is the rumination of food. They gather it with
their tongue or lips, cup it with their incisors, they chew it
slightly and then swallow. At which point it enters the larger
stomach occupying three quarters of the digestive system.
There the food, once fermented, enters the reticulum, where it
is separated into small bites and returned to the mouth again
where it is chewed, or ruminated, and mixed with saliva. Lastly
it is swallowed directly into the omasum, where digestion is
completed. This process of rumination isn't one that ruminants
learn the day they're born. Rather it begins the moment they
take their first food aside from milk.

the narrator says:

from the moment of separation
from the mother
they ruminate.

Rumination

within me words voiced
like dictation
when you dictate
and find the starting place
grasp the thread
and the flow begins
words following words
to speak then hesitate
catching it again
correcting it
smoothing it out
or making it even more feral
for effect
shaping it again
you ruminate
and all this voiced
loudly
up and down the room
and the next word comes
an image emerges
flashing before the eyes
then feeling
singular
to that moment
all of it is woven
and you want to say it
with words appropriate
in value to what was given you
and these are voiced
again taking shape and meaning
until the road runs out
rewilded

our steps bewildered
our decisions obsolete
until the trees the roots the branches
the buildings
seal the path
the faucet
stops!

Thanasis Koutinas transcribes a Vlach song:

Namisa si aceĺi doi muntsî	Between two mountains
Elu moi ana moi anamesa oreeee	He that goes between
Iara unǎ fǎntǎnǎ arace	There was a cold spring
Elu moi ana moi anamesa oreeee	He that goes between
Iara djone pliguitu	A young man with a wound
Elu moi ana moi anamesa oreeee	He that goes between
Tu tǎmpǎri avǎrtitu	Wrapped in a cape
Elu moi ana moi anamesa oreeee	He that goes between
Stu pǎrnari arucutitu	You birds that sing
Elu moi ana moi anamesa oreeee	He that goes between
Puiĺi tutsî lu virgǎrarǎ	In the fallen holly tree
Elu moi ana moi anamesa oreeee	He that goes between
Voi lǎi puĺi ci achiuratsî	All the birds enclose him
Elu moi ana moi anamesa oreeee	He that goes between
Tutu întregu s' nu mi mǎcatsî	Don't eat me completely
Elu moi ana moi anamesa oreeee	He that goes between
Mǎna îndreapta s' ńi alǎsatsî	Leave behind my right hand
Elu moi ana moi anamesa oreeee	He that goes between
Ta s' ǵrǎpsestu 'nǎ lai di carte	To write a black letter
Elu moi ana moi anamesa oreeee	He that goes between
Ta s' pitrecu la dada s' tate	For my mother and father
Elu moi ana moi anamesa oreeee	He that goes between
Ta s' mi plǎngǎ ta s' mi jiĺastǎ	So they know to mourn
Elu moi ana moi anamesa oreeee	He that goes between

Cyclops

I'm locked inside the cave of the Cyclops
with his solitary eye guarding me
I stay awake.
— Cyclops open the door for me!
— Cyclops let me leave!
the Cyclops caresses the fuzz on my back.
lights a fire
rubs his hands
eats my meat my cheese my wine
sleeps happily
still guarding me
burps
with his solitary eye open.

4. UTENSILS

Uncle Yannis: The goat wants it. I mean, really needs it, you know. It likes it. It's a comfort: the bell, all of it. Humans are the same way. We're no different.

Yannis Mavrakakis: The *kolevda* was a small satchel made from the shaved and sometimes tanned skin of the testicles and used by the shepherd as a cup for scooping water from the well or tank, and sometimes for drinking milk after milking, or filling from the milk jug. This and the *fouska* (bladder of a slaughtered animal) our shepherds used for holding tobacco.

Jakob Johann von Uexküll says:

The housefly, the dragonfly, and the bee we encounter in daylight do not move in the same world that we observe them from, nor share with us nor with each other the same time and space.

Giorgio Agamben says that Uexküll says:

We assign vague names to things we use or need, as if they were mere objects without relativity. No animal can be associated with an object like that.

> *Goatself:*
>
> I eat half a tub of yogurt
> and call Ivan over
> to eat the rest.
> it's small for such a big snout.
> he licks it carefully
> and a little tediously
> his tongue sideways
> along the rim struggling
> contorting to touch the bottom
> down the steep sides adapting
> his tongue to the vessel
> with no knowledge of geometry.

the shepherd calls:

pen (*stani*)
sheep-pen (*stanotopi*)
goat-pen sheep-*stani* cattle-pen horse-pen
dog-pen

staniazo: to put inside the pen
to take out of the pen *exstaniazo*
field-pen
Oldpen Penplace Narrowpen
devil-pen
beggar-pen
stud-pen
graiki: animal camp
stalos: stall, stalling-place—of ample noon shade
mantri: pound
mantra: paddock
mantroula: little paddock
gidomandri: goat-paddock.

the proverb says:

keep your males
from your females.

the narrator says:

fold for goats for milking.
fold for kids for slaughtering.
fold for babies kept alive in order to give birth.
fold for males to be let out
two weeks in the spring
so the females become pregnant in unison
and while pregnant climb the mountain.
and while pregnant climb back down.
timed so that in October
they give birth and on Christmas
the kids are slaughtered and in February
the second group is born and at Easter

they are slaughtered and in May
the males are shorn and on the first week of June
during cheese-making season
they go up the mountain in a truck.
the division of everything as it corresponds to human needs.
the division of time as it corresponds.
the division of space time work utility
as it corresponds to their needs.
factory or labor camp.

Loukopoulos says:

Stack-stack-stack, like that
they topple the tops of firs, cedars, anything,
and pile them up to make a fence,
and when winter comes?
The same again: entire branches of trees, oaks
and paliurus shrubs—taken for the fold
which sting us now, you see—
to build a pen for the young.

Loukopoulos again:

So, a fence all around the area, two openings,
the entrance to the front pen here, the stone used as a milking
            seat there,
and that's the *strougga.*
A traveling pen.
You just drag the branches along, set it up farther away,
whatever works.

"I put the animals inside the strougga"
"a man is strougged (penned)"

"some wild goats got in the strougga"
"animals unstrougged the shepherd"
"you fuck shit mother-pen"
"holy pen!"
"shit pen!"
"see how they destrougged my beautiful field"
"the strougga is wrecked" he said
when his teeth fell out of his mouth.
after all, don't the teeth make a pen
to enclose the captive tongue?

narrator:

strougga: some boards and chicken wire.
inside go the males for shearing
starting with the biggest.
strong animals with twisting horns. the leaders
wearing heavy bells of different tones—a dozen—
on which they play
the chromatic scale.
patterns shorn on their fur.
ancient lines and surfaces.
unshorn patches harvested fields.
along the fence plastic coffee cups
one goat stretches
its neck over the fence to place its lips
on a frappe straw and sips.
Terry the Albanian shepherd tells me:
"she likes it very much and I let her
because she's my little one."

Uncle Yannis says:

I shear 800 goats by myself!
Whenever I want to, see this pair of scissors here
I'm, you know, a fanatic.
Don't believe me? Take me anywhere, any camp,
I'll show you how I shear them
I do it my way, you see,
like a working man!
Only a craftsman can cut designs like this!
You can try it too—
see, you're doing it like the children do when they give them a
        haircut.

and Uncle Yannis says:

I even cut women's hair. Maroula, she comes to me and says,
"Cut my hair."
"Get out of here, you're a woman. How am I supposed to cut
        your hair?"
"Eh, come on, cut it."
So I cut it.
"How pretty," she says.

Joseph Dacre Carlyle and Philip Hunt say:

Small coins were tied into her braids, which fell down her back
        and nearly touched the ground.

Uncle Yannis says:

the same way you dress a woman, the headscarf,
the coins, and so on,
it's like that when you dress the herds.

From the large bells to the small bells, all to show off
in a way that's most, most presentable.
When I'm inspired, I dress the animals how I want.
Like you say, I want to give myself
a good appearance, that's what I do for the herd,
give it an appearance.

Ami Boué says:

The Greeks and Tsindari Vlachs will sometimes sing in chorus,
with one person making a nasal droning sound reminiscent of
the bagpipe. Their obsession with singing can sometimes be
unusual. Generally the flute is the accompanying instrument.
Everywhere in Greece, shepherds can be heard in the fields,
making wild melodies with their flutes to the gurgling of the
waters and the rustling of wind through the trees.

narrator:

wooden utensils, the traveler writes
carved art, the folklorist says
that which is carved.
crossing ravines and mountains collecting bits of wood.
wood for drinking cups for ladles wood for collars
spindle whorls.
wood for the wooden stake in the ground the rod.
wood for the shepherd's crook. for flutes.

Loukopoulos says:

the shepherd never lets
the crook slip from his hand
he would endure
what a boatman endures

who loses his oar
on the open sea
were you to take
the crook from his hands
he'd be rudderless
lost
which is why he sleeps
clutching it
day and night.

Archilochus says:

by my spear the bread
by my spear
the Ismaric wine
which I drink
leaning against it
by this spear
scaffolded.

Goatself:

what difference a crook and a spear?

Loukopoulos says:

curved crook of the shepherd carved from oak, wild olive
I took it up
I left it
I built my nest against it
hung from it
hung myself from it
it is all of my belongings.

Giorgis Exarchos writes:

However, Leake noticed some of the flutes from Epirus were unique and hadn't yet been recorded. They were made from the feet of eagles or griffon vultures, because their bones were very hard and long enough to be used for a shepherd's flute.

They are somewhat more common today than in the ancient world, because it is easier to kill a griffon vulture with gunpowder than, say, a bow.

Flutes

in a time of idleness,
when the tender breeze
Zephyr
blows and caresses
their cheeks,
they sit in the thick shade
of a rock.
drinking milk
or wine.
lulled by the rustle
of leaves
and the tiny song of the cicada.
carving wood
or whistling.
but the best flute
isn't made of wood
but from the bones
of an eagle.
to make this music
you first needed to learn
how to fly.

Hymn to Swallow and Nightingale

of the nightingale in the leaves

                                    hidden

its cry

                                    motionless

grieving in the morning and at night
each tree a nightingale   voice
in dialogue with others
in other trees

motionless cocking its head
to answer with its purring throat—

                            voicèd polyphony

with eyes fixated on the sky we seek

the extravagant the most unspoiled   and luminous
boughs the tender leaves
from our seats beneath the tree in the sunlight

though our view of the sky is clearer
the closer we are to the ground

                            lying on my back

I marvel at the celestial singer
while underneath in the yard
the stones carrying the day's trapped heat
warm me

                            it's getting late

the nightingale empties   the gladness
of the mouth   sounding
crying for its lost young
or a mate

boasting skyward with its outsized   voice
all but invisible
on the tallest branch

                        hovering

only *aman-aman*
mountain keening
voicings from the tender branches
shoot up
nourished by the waters of an invisible river

while the swallows sing only   in motion
when they fly they
scream midair
lacerate the blue   horizon
slash with their swordtails
the celestial   myriad

emitting shrill intermittent arrhythmic
joyful cries
grazing each other every now and then
as if to say
"my little swallow
there, in the distances where you reside."
we remain fastened to the land
while they
living creatures of the sky, flowers
in the air, toil away down our street
to build a single nest
each accompanying the other
with us   accompanied
they leave and return
leave and return

chitterings lullabies glidings
self-contained words   uttered
you of the unuttered   notes

swallow-reveling.

Sun and Night Stars

there is an observer narrator
there is my naked chest beneath the sun
the observer in present tense speaks in third person
for other beings
the sun singes, arouses
the observer speaks of the moon the glow of stars
the wind rain rain petals
crickets owls a cicada a fly
grass cherries mosquito
at times the narrator turns
and enters his words to confuse us
but I saw it: the white
shell of a cricket floating on the water surface
of the bucket in the garden
exoskeleton
illuminated by the sea and the stars of that particular
night
narrator it was yours, your old coat
your *geras* your cape your shield
tossed off, and from the fig tree
perched in the well's eye
to gaze at
your reflection

5. WORKS AND DAYS

Uncle Yannis: The Vlach Road was straight. We'd pass through Pelekoudi, Gerakari, Tsoukka, Deskati, then from there on to Dimitra—not Dimitra damnit, Karpero, and Christo, Kalpidi, and Grevena; the way was straight.

MM: Thirty-five days in the fall.

UY: In the spring it was seventeen.

MM: In the fall the animals weren't pregnant, and were trying to be more … economical.

UY: Seventeen days in the spring, versus thirty-five. Sometimes forty. One time in the road we did in forty days, an old man came out and said "forty days, eighty-five loaves."

MM: Loaves! From cracked wheat.

UY: Well, what bread we had we made into hardtack.

MM: We'd tear up the loaves and bake them again, into hardtack that would last for days. Forty days!

UY: But now we go up the mountain in trucks, as you see.

Aristotle says:

Which is why there are so many different types of animals and humans, and as it's impossible to live without food, the lives of animals differ depending on their food, and it's the same with humans. The nomadic are the most idle, because feeding their stock is nearly effortless, and when it is time to change pastures for them, they too must also follow, because they are cultivators of a living crop.

Léon Heuzey says:

The Vlach one meets in Acarnania is, on the contrary, the archetype of a nomad. Movement for him isn't an obligation he suffers, but a necessity, it is his life itself. I don't know what kind of spirit of change and motion courses the veins of the Vlach-Aromanians. Untethered from the soil where others stay as if rooted, where he's acquired, we might say, his nature from his herds that, every year, drive him up the mountains and back down into valleys. There's a common superstition among them, according to which if one of them were to settle down somewhere, and buy land and build a house, he'd soon grow sick and waste away, and become food for worms.

Henri Belle says:

Even on their mountains, in summer, while the women and children remain in their huts, the men wander the high plateaus with their dogs, changing their pastures each day and sleeping outdoors wrapped in woolen cloaks, indifferent to the sun, the rain, exhaustion, and hardship, living in a wild state in the company of hawks and. rocks, ignoring every progress and advance of civilization, scorning any other work, ignoring all but the money they receive from selling their goats and cheeses.

Pouqueville says:

They apportion time according to the phases of rural life, such as the kidding season, shearing time, and official religious holidays. On the feast day of Agios Georgios, which marks the start of the pastoral year, they celebrate with their families and eat roasted young goats that were born too early. The return of the swallows and the May nymph that blind minstrels sing to, traveling village to village, heralds the season of flowers and the florid days of April.

Chara says:

I walked through your door
you tried to play it off
but I could tell right away
you'd been eating garlic.

The song goes:

It is best to be a donkey in May
a ram in June
a cat in January
and a rooster always.

Uncle Yannis says:

A human life: if someone kept a diary from the day they're born till the last day, it would say, I lived. How could you argue with that? You couldn't say oh they lived like this, or had this specific life. No. It's bigger than that.

Henri Bell says:

In autumn, when the north wind brings the first snows as a
harbinger of heavy winter to come, they descend back down
into the valleys. In spring, when the scorching heat that is fatal
to the animals begins, and the young goats have been sold for
Easter, they slowly ascend back into the cold airs from which
winter had driven them.

Stamatia, on the train to Athens, says:

a very mixed autumn this year for us
sometimes clouds sometimes light rain
maybe that's why it's snowing now
this year we had a very mixed autumn
at Christmas there were days
that felt like Easter

you don't know what the wind was like that wind
brought down all the trees
tore our tarps
so I'm rushing around
and manage to save up eight containers this year

in winter if you don't have a reason don't travel

what nature provides is good
change is good
everyone needs change
what's your name?
my name is Stamatia

usually I travel at night
so I can be home by morning
I have a little girl
she carries a bag soooo big
the bottom of her feet are swollen
like bread

I really like to get home the night before
to air out the house, to cook

you're by yourself every day, no?
why not be on holiday too?

they say:

when the moon sleeps
the shepherd stays awake.

When the moon is up
the shepherd sleeps.

Passov recorded the song "Sea Bird and Mountain Bird":

a bird from the sea and a bird from the mountain
were fighting, were fighting
for the mountain, the pasture, the shore;
the sea bird says to the mountain bird:
"Go back to your place, bird, go back to your people.
I've put up with you too long, I won't do it anymore."
"Don't yell at me, bird, stop trying to shoo me away,
I'm only staying here a little while.
Perhaps May through June and July

and maybe five days in August or maybe six or ten,
then I'm off, back home to my own."

Pouqueville says:

The bleating of the goats, the yelps of the dogs, and the shouts
and banging of the shepherds gave a special music to this
moving phalanx of people and animals from Pindos to the
valleys of Macedonia and Thessaly.

    Like the storks, those famous migrating birds that travel
far from their home and their nests, taking their new families
with them over lands and seas, the Vlachs push onwards with
the hope that next year they'll once again find their homes and
those they left behind.

the narrator (spring equinox on a bus on the highway):

again the yellow fields
the heavy heat the farm machinery the olives
shining in wind
Misko numero 1 in Greece
light in columns and shafts from gray
clouds bearing rain
the summer water
thunder smells of earth
LINET industries
Assos boilers
Stasinopoulos Timber Formica
BLK Aluminum
Rouchotas Timber Parquet
corn
Rough-Hewn Marble
oil drums

and now rain
a shepherd holding his crook
off the highway
white oleander blossoms
cimarelli cimarelli
olive shakers
dense cornfields
butcher-slash-taverna
Krokio Public School
gas station
fields road and sea
wood pellets coal
wall of corn
corn barley for sale
prepackaged or in bulk
river bends
and now bridge
figs reeds and plane trees
rest stop
garden bed with veggies
harvested field
boustrophedon
mom said to get sweet acacia for the house
Locker Room
and vineyards
Pelion Stone Hearths
The Reunion Bar & Grill
blue tiles on the wall
Organic Vineyards or KTEO
AIPE gas station
nameless gas station
unknown gas station

Volos 20 kilometers
animal feed oleander
sweet acacia and mulberry she told me
but the roots don't fit anywhere

Yannis Tsevrechos says:

The goats are incompatible with the enclosure's stale air, so
they stare out through the slats. Even in winter, no matter how
bad the weather gets, the goat wants to see it for itself, even if it
can only stand half an hour outside. Even if it has everything it
needs, food and water, inside.

Pouqueville says:

We saw long lines of sheep and goats, followed by a solitary
shepherd playing the flute and walking behind.

the breeder says:

They have developed a sense of navigation I tell you, if you
leave them somewhere, they can get back again, they know
how to move in a way that finds the path of least resistance,
the clear path, they read a place, its geography, they're in sync
with nature, born in nature. This we saw but never experienced
ourselves, which is why we changed professions.

Joseph Dacre Carlyle and Philip Hunt say:

Walking in the street with their swaddled babies on their backs,
balancing a large jar or urn on their heads while all the time
twining the distaff, winding the spindle.

Demetris Letsios the photographer says:

We traveled on foot and at night on the way to Agrafa because during the day there were airplanes. We walked through the fields at night. But this life was also good. The role played by women in the fields during the resistance was important.

Apostolos Bardas says:

we Vlachs are like birds
come March and April and we're gone
mountainward.

Vlach proverb:

Τάστουρλου ντι-ν-ανούμιρα σι φούγγα.
(Bag on the shoulder and go.)

Morning Epilogue

this summer.
I lived with loved ones.
I walked in the forest.
this summer.
we didn't swim in the sea
but entered it and sat for hours
talking while rotating our feet
just enough to float.
we climbed on the horses
went berry picking
let time pass as it wanted
without forcing.
Ivan
our new dog brought us here.
after I'd finished
L'esprit du Zen
the first and last book
of the summer
Ivan stole it like he does
tore it apart with his teeth.
pages leaves bits of fragments
text
drifted across the yard
carried off by wind.
I kept trying to grab them
as they were leaving.
how to walk in the spirit of zen?
how to move through the world
coherently
when all your verbs
are past tense
and the stars that you see

went out an eternity ago.
the loss—possession
the past—belonging to now
as memory to oblivion.
the almond between your teeth is earth.

Morning Hot and Windless

spread out along the olive tree like a drawn bow.
my back against the tree
my abdomen against the sky
hands uplifted
feet open to winds
suspended in the world
while everywhere the endless drone
of cicadas in chorus
alone I strove away from the others
for hours splitting the air
with my strange and sad desire's
keen.
o sea of olives and noonday stone
above the bright sea of goats out
to the shining Aegean
farther out
to the horizon's secret end.

6. CHIMERA

Yannis Mourtos: You saw why I was there for the birth. I was pulling out the goat. Step by step.

This love, my little one. Like nothing in life.

the narrator says:

I was still little when I saw a cow giving birth
on the steep slopes of the mountain
saw the eyes
as soon as it left the womb
shining with fluids
trembling it stood on its thin legs
for human children it takes a year to walk.

Yannis Mourtos says:

After it happened to me, I mean since I learned about birth,
how animals give birth, there in the tractor the woman gave
birth, I cut the cord a little longer and tied it with the string
from a pompom hanging from the mirror.

Makis Mourtos says:

Don't be shocked by what he says about a woman giving birth
on the route. In those days most women gave birth that way.
On the route. They set out from here for seventeen to twenty
days at a time, and if a woman was pregnant and far along,
she'd give birth on the route. There was no hospital to go to, or
anything else.

narrator:

Sometimes there are new mothers who don't want the baby.
They won't feed them. To discipline the mothers they remove
them from the flock. They confine them for one or two days in
a 5' x 5' enclosure with their kids. Till they get used to it, and
are forced to give their milk.

Transhumance I

for Eleonora and Dimitris

It was I who sent
my treasure
by my own free will
silently I step upon the earth

i.
In the beginning was the grazing
the pasture, sections of earth gathered extended
suffused from rain and the elements
eaten
by footsteps, the cursive of animals and humans
echoing
the valleys, streams, and summits beyond
brought back voices.

ii.
In the beginning was the field.
To move out I had to gather.
I had to cull
the things.
The things, the animals, the things, the things.

iii.
— What do you carry on you when you leave?
— My dark. My own piece of dark.
— What do you carry when you leave?
— The markings on the body.
— What do you carry when you leave?
— My spell:
Forgot–tenacts–forgot–tenwords
fragme–ntsof–theform–erlife
tokeep–ascharm–tokeep–asnew–redcru–cifix.

iv.
—To move on I had to cull
the things, the fragments
my children
left behind
before leaving me to begin their own lives.

v.
— *Kiatra kraapa omlou nou kriapa*
(A stone breaks, a man does not break.)

vi.
— Still
the fragments are glass
pressed deep under skin
traveling in the flesh
choosing their own paths,
one ascends to the heart,
another pierces your abdomen.

— What does God cast down that the earth does not swallow?
— Wound through and through.
I spit it from my mouth like a bitter seed
but not a single teardrop touched my cheek,
why I had for years now
clenched my teeth.

— You cannot eat a stone, mother says
instead of
you cannot escape your fate.
— In order to leave
I had to cull the things.

That agony lasted months.
An entire winter.
Heavy and dark, stripping layer by layer
the vessels of memory.
But what hurt most
was what had, for so long, slipped
between my fingers like air.
What had been forgotten.
The missing.
What had not happened.

— Λεῦσσε δ' ὅμως ἀπεόντα νόῳ παρεόντα βεβαίως

Parmenides says:

but see with your mind those who are missing, as if
they were present.

vii.
—And the upbringing was over. the departure performed.
absence a native plant sprouting
separation a self-growing pain
seed without water roots in secret
distance-nurtured
what you didn't do hurts more
than what was done
spring arrives. for a moment the darkness
is paused.
and I can leave. lighter.
I carried as little as possible
most I left behind in rooted houses.
of motherhood.
my home is transient.

I carry with me only a few boxes
fragments of the former life
pictures and writings
for use in
my solitary
ceremony
of unbinding tears.

viii.
To leave I had to gather the things
beneath my feet the earth was leaving
it takes time to uproot from one's place.
it takes time to leave a life's worth of wrappers.
it takes time to disentangle from your children's roots.
but you don't.
I made the wrong association.
children's things equal the children themselves
who've left.
uprooted already. what I keep is mine.
you said: don't throw them away, they're memories.
(and I believed you'd remain small always believed
the moment would stay)
and you kept: broken toys bits of paper
cards and tickets pictures magazines
fragments
books a ceramic pot you once painted
a tin box filled with paper
a piggy bank shaped like a red bus
plastic dragons soldiers torn posters
more dragons. paintings of dragons.
pieces stuck to the wall.
and you kept: photographs of actors
pen sketches on notebook paper

pictures of your summer vacation
your favorite band which changed and changed again
a model with a huge bag that read:
"I never find what I'm looking for"
a scrap of paper that said *only love matters*
that you taped to the wardrobe.
the bedroom walls were friezes
triglyphs and metopes
ornamented
with your own mythos
apotropaic charms against fear
ornament of intimacy.
I took them down one by one.
some so old they tore.
some I put in the box.
the walls stripped naked.
and painted for the next tenants.
new traces applied to them.
nothing will say what the house was for us
or what unknown beautiful children grew up
in it.
to move on I had to throw your things away.

ix.
To move on I had to gather my things.
to remember to consider I had to think
to abandon.
what I could gather I gathered
what I could keep I kept
time can't repeat no going back to live it again
at this task I was properly lost.
wounded.
mother is a wound.

x. *Wish*
I cry just two times a year now
it starts when I'm asleep
you're small and tender and cool to the touch
like water
and when I wake I'm already crying
because you've grown
how far you are now.
may your heart always remain tender
in your large body.
and your life be long
and lucky and joyful.
"with my blessing," grandma would say
when we told her goodbye. go.

Noon

for El

I heard your voice
upstairs. there's a scorpion
in the bathroom.
and picked out
a fat tome
The Neverending Story
from the bookshelf
of the orphanage: what you and your friends called
that cramped chamber
with its two single beds and little icon
on the headboard,
and hurled it at him.
we stomped on the cover
again and again
until the life was gone.
always
my daughter
you are the one to find them.
you'd seen it years ago
in the darkness near the spring
beside the plane trees and cistern
the giant scorpion.
the bitterness of its venom drawn to sweetness.
wishing to join in a single word.
bittersweet.
mother's daughter
rushing water.
when the Kore uproots
gone from the earth
of Demeter. of the mother.

7. SACRIFICE

Uncle Yannis: You see. Man is a beast. If he wants something, he takes it. Because now, with the crisis, the one who wants to get ahead will get ahead. The one who doesn't, never will.

Goatself:

river full of stars will you hear me?
I came down the ridge to speak to you,
along the shores of your tributaries spiders
dance
weaving unraveling life
dance of unraveling wherein Athena
faces Dionysus.

the narrator:

a goat gave birth to a dead kid
in its place they gave her a sheep
a sheep growing up amongst goats
won't have a good fate,
says the goatherd.

Goatself:

I remember watching you
as you were going down the ridge
when the bells were ringing all at once
like a voice
of one accord.

the narrator elaborates:

he bisects the throat with a knife
cuts with a handsaw the horns
inserts a tube
through a hole between the skin and the flesh
inflates it with a pump

to begin separating with his fingers skin from flesh
he cuts away the front extremities
folds the skin inside out
removes the hide from the back feet (now upwards)
towards the head (downwards now)
the knife reaches the head, pares away the skin
from the cheeks the mouth the ears
with one last flick he dissevers it and tosses it aside
suspending the pelt on the hook by the tendons of the feet

his is an absolute precision he is the dancer

bisects with the knife from throat to clavicle
bisects vertically the stomach in the middle
tugs out the large intestine tosses it aside
tugs out the viscera the hearts stomachs all together.
— how little were you when you learned to do this?
— very little. Look, it's best to learn it all when you're very
            little.
Rips the abdomen and tugs out the heart the viscera
coils the intestine in a spool,
sets aside a piece of stomach for the rennet,
cuts the head,
halves the body end to end
whatever lands on the ground
is food for the chickens and dogs
from each half he cuts away the feet
cutting the ribs one by one
in motions of absolute precision he is the dancer.

Homer says:

and near us the goatherd Melanthius passed by
leading the finest goats
from each herd to give a feast
for the suitors,
and two shepherds followed him.

Walter Burkert on sacrifice in ancient Greece:

the blood must never touch the ground
if the animal is small, they hoist it above the altar,
or else collect its blood in a designated vessel
and with it anoint the altar stone
which must at all times ceaselessly leak blood.
The animal is cut in sections and its viscera removed.
The uses for each portion
are strictly determined by tradition.
First they place the still-beating heart on the altar.
A seer is always on hand
to read the lobes of the liver.
Quickly they scorch the guts in the altar's flame
and devour them piping hot.
Only the gallbladder is left uneaten.
Meanwhile the femurs
along with the pelvis and the tailbone
are laid on the altar "in orderly fashion."
The arrangement of the bones indicates
their interrelation
the members of the living animal
and its primary form is restored
as sacrifice.

Homer says:

And now they laughed as though from lips not their own
bloodstained from the meat they had eaten, their eyes
filled with tears, and in their minds it was as if they were
                grieving.

Regarding those who are buried without a funeral, Exarchos offers:

After the day of execution people heard frequently,
around the time of midnight, voices, the cries
and screams of the fighters:
—*Ouleleleleee, oulelele, oulelelelleleleee...*

Overheard among the shepherds:

— the number of males you keep depends on the size of your
            herd, for each male there must be a certain number of
            females.
— how many females for 15 males?
— about five times that.
— ah, five times.
— one male suffices for twenty females.
— one male twenty females.

            Goatself:

            its eyes still bleary the newborn goat
            is searching for my finger to suck
            my finger
            and heart
            are glad.

and later we will drink
its mother's milk
meant for it.

the shepherd says:

when the children leave the mothers grieve.

Transhumance II

for mom

i.
words are markings on the mountains
the mountains aren't spoken
the words are plaited tracks
the words are branches
the place flashes through time
time does not exist
time turns back
each year I ascend and descend your line
time
carrying nothing on my back
I stitch I unravel joy through sorrow
carrying each day on my back.

ii.
in the beginning was the law: scraps of earth allotted
how far? up to the markings
each time a little farther out
beyond.

iii.
boats of people leave in droves
young and strong
their mothers in their headscarves left behind
wondering "where are you now, my son?"
daily and praying
in the light,
will they find out in the end?
"where are you, my son," the goddess Thetis asks,
a cuttlefish or cormorant
diving into the sea
like a bird in the sky

"I nursed you with rosewater
raised you with milk
with my immortal fire
I submerged you within it
to be a shield for your body for when you're beyond my reach
but bodies are bodies, they're tangible
and I had to hold you by the ankles
upside down
from your tiny heels
and this stamp this undying grip
became your vulnerable marking, my dear
the place of the mother's grip
the mark of death."

iv.
they called and said
come over
when I got there a young shepherd
stood inside the pen a tall redhead
in a cobalt blue uniform choosing
kids for slaughter
males mostly, two months old
he took them one by one in his arms
and while they bleated walked over
cross dangling over his chest
and carried them across the fence
to the other side
he was Christ and Calf Bearer
and Charon
but also he was midwife
and mother he knew
by heart whose child was which

having guided with his hands
each one's mouth to its mother's breast
he showed it how
and even taught the mother
what to do
now he shoves each one inside
the black opening of the truck bed
the mouth that would
take them to Hades
and when
one manages to nudge
its tiny head through the hole he stops
to caress
it lovingly before hitting
its nose back in
when the mothers return to the pen
from pasture
and find them gone
inconsolable—he tells me—they grieve
do they realize?
will they remember?

Darkness Again

for years the dead didn't bother us
we tucked them one by one into the earth
from which
often the most recent
would visit us
usually in our sleep and without warning
empty-handed
like memory's beggars
their gaze and voice
and sudden appearance
at our door
were sometimes frightening
other times comforting
gradually emptiness tugged them
beyond reach
always further and further out
merging with the nonexistent
remnants
of an enveloping cosmos
of which we know nothing
or can even conceive
far shadows of a dream
that we forgot
but never once
did their blood stop reaching
still deeper
through the same quirks, the same demeanor
and forgotten antics
that belonged to us,
or were they theirs alone?
for years the dead didn't bother us
then the pains began

and love
which woke them and made them
reach out their hands again
to us and night
to their song from nowhere
their own nowhere inside
our here and now
blood, earth, flesh, bone,
and joint heart abiding.

the cantor says:

each action each thought each state of each being
that passed through the world
does it exist now and always?
do they raise into the sky like hands like branches
voices coalescing repeating from their first hour
of utterance?
does each one's walking or swimming
or moving through the air sound in unison
from the first, unchanging?
are new voices yet added
to their song?
we return to find
the ones who come
over and over with weapons without weapons
with another step another hoof fall
the beauty of the virgins
in the battle of Alcman.

from the General State Archives:

ANSWER: One night, three days before being discharged, slaves entered the village Sourpi, and the three of us, thieves, were staying around the village and went into the houses and took bread. [...] In the evening we went down again and were given food by the Karvouno Vlachs and stayed among the sheepfold in a place I don't know the name of.

QUESTION: Why have you taken up a life of thievery?

ANSWER: To become rich.

QUESTION: You know how to read and write?

ANSWER: I know, yes, but I cannot sign because my hand is wounded and in pain.

Notes

Donna Haraway (U.S. philosopher, biologist, eco-feminist)

Léon Heuzey (French traveler, archaeologist, historian, 1831–1922)

Homer (ancient Greek epic oral poets going as back as far as a millennium BCE, transcribed in a written version centuries later, perhaps in the 6th century BCE)

Ivan (the narrator's dog)

Panagiotis Karakanas (Vlach cheese maker in Volos)

Maria Kokkinou and Andreas Kourkoulas (Greek architects)

Thanasis Koutinas (singer and teacher of Vlach polyphony)

William Martin Leake (British traveler, military officer and classical scholar, topographer of ancient cities, 1777–1860)

Dimitris Letsios (member of the Greek resistance to the Nazis and photographer from Volos, 1910–2008)

Henry George Liddell (1811–1898) and Robert Scott (1811–1887) (British classical scholars, authors of *A Greek-English Lexicon,* first published in 1843)

Dimitris Loukopoulos (Greek folklorist from Roumeli, 1874–1943)

Iris Lykourioti (Greek architect and designer)

Yannis Mavrakakis (Cretan folklorist, 1940–2021)

Mother (Kaiti Giannisi)

Andreas Moukas (Greek breeder, Mount Parnassus, voice recording from the Melpo and Octave Merlier Archive)

Makis Mourtos (MM, Yannis Mourtos' nephew, ex-breeder from Aetomilitsa-Denitsko)

Narrator

Yannis Mourtos (UY or Uncle Yannis, breeder, goat-herd owner from Aetomilitsa, seventy years old)

Parmenides (Greek pre-Socratic philosopher and poet, c. 515–c. 450 BCE)

Arnold Passov (German Hellenist who collected Greek folk songs, 1829–1870)

Plato (ancient Greek philosopher from Athens, c. 428– c. 348 BCE)

François Charles Hugues Laurent Pouqueville (French traveler, diplomat, explorer, physician, 1770–1838)

Stamatia (a train passenger)

Chara Stergiou (Greek architect, artist)
Thetis (mythic mother of the hero Achilles and a goddess of the sea)
Yannis Tsevrechos (from the village of Diasello in Thessaly, a
    goatherd, author of *The Flock*)
Giorgos Tzirtzilakis (Greek art curator, critic, and historian)
Jakob Johann Freiherr von Uexküll (Baltic German biologist, 1864–
    1944)
Alan John Bayard Wace (1879–1957) and Maurice Scott Thompson
    (1884–1971) (British archaelogists, authors of *The Nomads of the
    Balkans,* 1914)
X and X2 (goatherds)
You

ETYMOLOGY

Goatself is a name given by a former teacher combining "ego (I)" and
its homophone "*aigo* (goat)." If the etymology of "ego" is "edo" (here),
a place implying "me," then Goatself signifies a multiplicity of beings
that live in this place and share the speaker's voice.

Nomad: member of a people traveling from place to place to find
pasture for its animals. More generally, a wanderer. In plural: pastoral
tribes, also of the Cyclopes. From the Greek νομ-άς , άδος, ὁ, ἡ, the one
that is roaming about for pasture. Comes from the verb νέμω (nemo),

    I.   distribute, share, allot, distribute in groups
    II. generally, enjoy
    III. recite
    IV. of herdsmen, pasture, to graze their flocks, drive to pasture

As also νόμος, ὁ (nomos)
    I.   usage, custom
    II. melody, strain
    III. in modern Greek: law

Song (tragoudi), n.

   I.   a canticle, small goat. From *tragodia*, tragedy, goat song: a Chorus consisting of Goats.

Tragedy (tragoudia), f.

   I.   the dramatic genre that flourished in ancient Athens during the fifth century, structured in various parts. It combined verses, song, music, and orchestration, and was performed as an official religious and political event in the theatre of Dionysus by an all-male Chorus and by citizens of Athens as actors. According to Aristotle, its purpose was to make the audience feel strong emotions of pity and fear, culminating in catharsis.

   II.   a work that belongs to that genre.

   III.   a modern theatrical work that has a sad story.

   IV.   (concurrently) a tragic event.

Instead of tragedy, Aigedy.

From *aix, aigos* (αἴξ , αἰγός, ὁ, ἡ) :

   I.   *goat*, mostly fem.,

   II.   αἴξ Ἄγριος wild *goat*

   III.   plural, *waves*

The Aegean Sea (*ΑΙΓΑΙΟ ΠΕΛΑΓΟΣ*) is derived from *aix*, and so is *Kataigis* (the storm).

PROVERBS

"goats are plough-free": for those who have been relieved of some weight (because the free nature of goats makes it impossible for them to be attached to ploughs)

"to the wild goats" : to the crow (to hell)

"goat names": of worthless objects.

Names of goats according to their color:

Arapou
Aspronourou
Flora
Florakanouto
Floro
Gaitanou
Galani
Geso
Giosa
Gormpo
Griva
Kanouta
Kanouto
Kavrelou
Kokkia
Kokkinomata
Koula
Laggonou
Laia
Liara
Liaro
Liopra
Matoulou
Mavri
Mavrokefalo
Mavrosfaiki
Melani
Mourakia
Mourna
Mouschro
Mouskouri
Mpalia
Mpaliatsoukou
Mpartsa

Mpartzo

Mpellia

Mpellou

Mpoutska

Paliri

Pestra

Podarousio

Prentzia

Psaria

Reikou

Rousa

Rouso

Spakou

Tsoukou

Vakrakia

Zarkad

Zonou

Names of goats according to their horns:

Klourokerato

Koutsokera

Krouta

Monokerati

Mproustoukera

Pisokera

Siouta

Stifanoukera

Striftokera

Traousio

Tsapaloukera

Tsiougka

Names of goats according to their udders:

Apalarmechti

Fouradomastari

Kalamoviza
Kalamovrizou
Kountoumastari
Koutlomastari
Makriviza
Mounouviza
Sfichtarmechti
Tsimporoviza
Tsimprovizou
Xountrouviza

According to their ears:

Lagofites
Mpalouchtres
Tsoupres

And more names for goats:

Apokonto
Arfani
Diplares
Falakri
Grammatou
Koutsounourla
Krouta
Ksanthoprosopi
Lagou
Lefka
Liafta
Liventou
Makraftou
Miksiasmeno
Mita
Morfou
Moukla
Mourka

Mouroucheiliasmeni
Mpafoukiasmeno
Mparezou
Mpovoulou
Niatou
Ntrenia
Palioflora
Paliogormpa
Paliokanouta
Pianoumenh
Tsimpidou
Virgi

Yannis Tsevrechos says:

Women used to lose their names
since the world called them
by the name of their husband.

Acknowledgments

Grateful acknowledgment is made to the following
publications in which some of these translations first appeared:

Asymptote, "Prelude: Gray March Sky," "Transhumance I"
Denver Quarterly, "Noon," "Hymn to Swallow and Nightingale"
Guernica, "Noon"
Modern Poetry in Translation, "Noon"
Poetry, "Morning Hot and Windless," "Rumination"
The Southern Review, "Morning Epilogue"
World Literature Today, "Cyclops"

Chimera was funded in part by a National Endowment for the
Arts Literature Translation Fellowship.

Thanks to all the Vlach goat herders of Kalamaki Larisis who
opened their pens and accepted the Goatself and Narrator's
presence, even in delicate moments, such as the mass birth
delivery: mainly Yannis, Makis, Miltos, and Nikos Mourtos,
and also Tasos Lagas and Lefteris Digos. Because *Chimera* is
literally a polyphonic and multilingual work, which had to
be shortened in size, the translation and editing of the project
were particularly difficult and time-consuming. Goatself
would like to express her gratitude to both the translator
Brian Sneeden for undertaking the arduous effort and all his
wonderful work once more, and to editor Declan Spring for
his patience, his careful reading of many different versions,
and his decisive contribution at all stages of the publication.
Marian Bantjes also contributed with her incredible design
work. And finally: to Goatself's dear friends Stathis Gourgouris,
a poet himself, and Michaeljohn Raftopoulos, an architect
and cautious reader, for their immense help and contributing
remarks regarding the English-language versions of the

work. And since this is (among other things) a book about companionship, Goatself shall remember, nor could she forget, her partner Zissis Kotionis, for sharing together bread and wine.

This project appeared previously in various forms: in several poetic performances, an exhibition with Iris Lycourioti (*AIGAI_O: The Songs*, Aggeliki Chatzimichali Museum, Athens, 2015), and a performance lecture in the Antigone Onassis Festival (*Nomos: The Land Song*, New York, 2016), directed by Isabella Martzopoulou.

Phoebe Giannisi is the author of eight collections of poetry, including *Chimera* (Kastaniotis, 2019), and most recently, *Thetis and Aedon* (Kastaniotis, 2021). A 2016 Humanities Fellow of Columbia University, Giannisi is a professor of architecture at the University of Thessaly, and coeditor of the literary journal *FRMK*. She has translated Ancient Greek lyric poetry as well as the poetry of Barbara Koehler, Gregor Laschen, Jesper Svenbro, and André Pieyre de Mandiargues. She lives in Volos, Greece.

Brian Sneeden is the author of *Last City* (Carnegie Mellon, 2018). His poetry and translations have received the *Iowa Review* Award in Poetry, an NEA Literature Translation Fellowship, the *World Literature Today* Translation Award for Poetry, the Constantinides Memorial Translation Prize, a PEN/Heim Translation Grant, and other recognitions. His translation of Phoebe Giannisi's *Homerica* was published by World Poetry Books in 2017, and his translation of Giannisi's collection *Cicada* was published by New Directions in 2022. He is a lecturer in English at Manchester Metropolitan University.